THE PHOTO DICTIONARY
OF THE
ORCHESTRA

THE PHOTO DICTIONARY
OF THE
ORCHESTRA

Melvin Berger

(n) METHUEN, New York

Library of Congress Cataloging in Publication Data
Berger, Melvin.
The photo dictionary of the orchestra.

SUMMARY: An alphabetically arranged, cross-
referenced dictionary of orchestra terms illustrated
with photographs and including definitions of the
instruments, the instrument groups, and the personnel
that make up an orchestra.
1. Orchestra—Juvenile literature. 2. Musical
instruments—Juvenile literature. [1. Orchestra.
2. Musical instruments] I. Title.
ML3930.A2B499   785'.06'610321   80-15134
ISBN 0-416-30681-0

Published in the United States of America by
Methuen, Inc.
733 Third Avenue
New York, N.Y. 10017

For Nathan Gottschalk and the Chautauqua Music
School Festival Orchestra, and Ronald Schweitzer
and the National Orchestra Association.

ACKNOWLEDGMENTS

The author wishes to thank Nathan Gottschalk, conductor, and the members of the Music School Festival Orchestra of the Chautauqua Institution (Robert R. Hesse, President), and Ronald Schweitzer, conductor, and members of the National Orchestral Association (Lois Schweitzer, Executive Director) for allowing him to photograph them at rehearsals and concerts, and to reproduce the photographs in this book.

THE PHOTO DICTIONARY
OF THE
ORCHESTRA

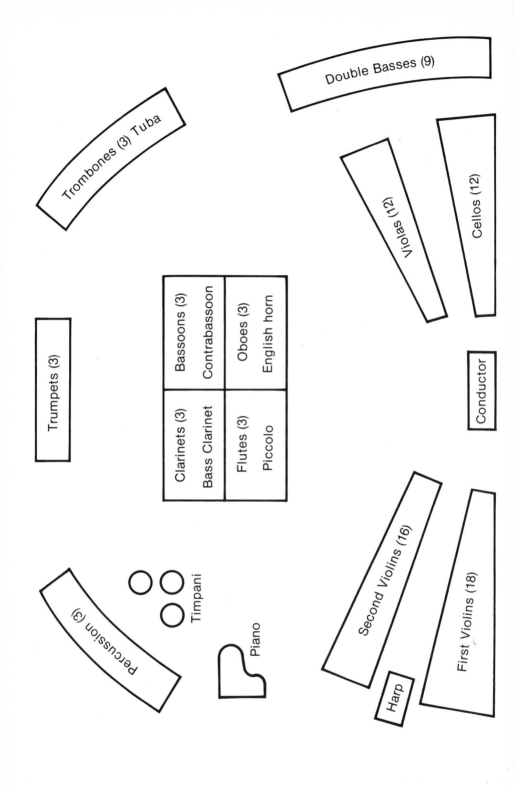

MEET THE ORCHESTRA

An orchestra is a group of musicians who play together under the direction of a conductor. The word orchestra was first used by the ancient Greeks to mean the space in the theaters between the stage and the audience where the chorus sang and danced. The first orchestras, in the modern sense of the word, date from around the year 1600. The players in these orchestras sat in front of the stage to accompany performances of the early operas. Over the following years, orchestras grew in size and importance. Gradually they began to give concerts by themselves, on stages, before large audiences.

There are nearly 30 different instruments in a modern full symphony orchestra. They are divided into four groups: strings (violins, violas, cellos, double basses); woodwinds (flutes, oboes, clarinets, bassoons); brasses (trumpets, French horns, trombones, tubas); and percussion (timpani, drums, cymbals, triangle). In addition to these main instruments in each group, there are others that may also be included. Among them are the harp, piccolo, English horn, bass clarinet, contrabassoon, saxophone, piano, and any number of percussion instruments.

No two kinds of instruments are alike in size, construction, or manner of playing. Yet basically they are all alike in the way that they produce sound. Each instrument sounds when the player sets something into very fast back and forth movement, called vibration. In the string instruments, the player sets the stretched strings into vibration by stroking them with a bow or plucking them with a finger. In the woodwinds, the player blows past a reed or across a hole in the tube, which sets the air inside into vibration. In the brasses, the player's lips start the air vibrating within the instrument. And in the percussion, the vibrations are caused by hitting or shaking the various instruments.

By controlling the vibrations, the player is able to change the pitch sounded by the instrument. Pitch refers to how high or low a note sounds. It is caused by the speed of vibration. The faster the speed, the higher the pitch; the slower the speed, the lower the pitch.

For most instruments, the players change the pitch by lengthening or shortening the vibrating part of the instrument, which changes the vibrating speed. In the string instruments, the player presses the fingers of the left hand on the strings. In the woodwinds, the player covers or opens holes along the tube, either with a finger or by pressing a key. In the brasses, the player presses a valve, or in the trombone, moves a slide. Harp, piano, xylophone, and glockenspiel players change pitch by setting strings or slabs of various lengths into vibration, using a different one for each note. And the timpani player changes pitch by tightening or loosening the head of the instrument.

A full symphony orchestra has about 100 musicians. But there are also orchestras with fewer players. There are pit orchestras that play for operas, ballets, and musical shows, which may only have 30 or 40 players. There are chamber orchestras with most of the same instruments as a symphony orchestra, but with fewer players in each section. And there are string orchestras, which only include string instruments, and seldom number more than 20 players.

At the head of almost every orchestra is a conductor. The conductor decides where the members of the orchestra are to be seated. Most conductors place the strings on the front side of the stage. The violins are to the conductor's left, and the violas, cellos, and double basses are to the right. The woodwinds are near the center of the stage, just behind the strings. The brass and percussion instruments are arranged across the back of the stage.

The orchestra holds a number of rehearsals before each concert, with the conductor in charge. In front of the conductor is a full score that shows each of the player's parts. The conductor uses a short stick, called a baton, to lead the musicians through the program, starting and stopping and keeping the group together by means of various hand and arm gestures. The conductor and players work together to correct any mistakes and to get the exact sounds and effects the composer asked for in the score.

The end result of the rehearsals is, of course, the concert. The musicians follow the conductor's beats to play together. They respond to the conductor's movements to achieve the correct mood and expression. Together, conductor and players make each note in the score come alive for the pleasure and entertainment of the audience.

Whether you go to concerts, listen to orchestras on records, radio, or television, play in an orchestra, plan to study an instrument, or just want to know more about orchestras, *The Photo Dictionary of the Orchestra* is for you. You can read it like a regular book, or you can use it to look up words or terms connected with the orchestra. The many candid photographs of orchestras in rehearsal and in concert and the short text tell you about the musicians and instruments that make up an orchestra. Knowing more about the orchestra will enrich your musical life and make listening to music or playing an instrument more fun.

BASS. *See* Double Bass

BASS CLARINET
The lowest sounding member of the clarinet family. The bass clarinet is longer and thicker than the standard clarinet, and its range extends eight notes lower. It has a curved metal neck and a metal bell that faces up. The sound is produced by a single reed. A symphony orchestra usually includes just one bass clarinet.

BASS DRUM. *See* Drums

BASSOON

The largest and lowest woodwind instrument. The bassoon is also called a fagot, which means a bundle of sticks. Actually the instrument is an eight-and-a-half-foot (2.6-meter) hollow tube that is doubled over into a U-shape to make it only four feet (1.2 meters) tall. The sound is produced by a double reed placed at the end of a curved metal tube, called a crook. The reed is held between the lips, and when the player blows, the two reeds vibrate against each other to make the sound. Sometimes called the clown of the orchestra, the bassoon is frequently used in playing humorous music. A full symphony orchestra has two or three bassoons plus one contrabassoon.

A bassoonist dries out each section of the instrument before putting it back into its case. Pulling a cloth through the tube absorbs moisture and prevents the wood from splitting.

BASS VIOL. *See* Double Bass

BATON. *See* Conductor

BOW
Used to set the strings of the string instruments into vibration. A modern violin bow consists of a 30-inch (76-centimeter) stick of Pernambuco wood. Stretched across this stick are about 200 hairs, either horsehair or a plastic substitute. The player uses a screw device at the end of the bow to loosen or tighten the bow hairs.

The cello bow is heavier and shorter than the violin bow.

BRASS

The family of blowing instruments that includes the trumpet, French horn, trombone, and tuba. Brass instruments are made of a mixture of copper and zinc. Each one has a separate cup-shaped mouthpiece that supports the player's buzzing lips, which actually produce the sound. The tighter the lips, the faster the vibrations and the higher the pitch; the slower the vibrations, the lower the pitch. Pitch is also determined by length of tubing. For the trumpet, French horn, and tuba, the player presses valves to lengthen or shorten the tubing. For the trombone, the player moves the slide in or out. The shorter the length, the higher the pitch; the longer the length, the lower the pitch. There are 12 to 15 brass players in a typical orchestra. They sit towards the back of the stage, usually in the center and to the conductor's right.

Trumpets

French Horns

Trombones

Tuba

CASTANETS

Small, shell-shaped wooden clappers in the percussion family of instruments. The name means small chestnut in Spanish and refers to the shape of the castanets. When used by orchestra players, the castanets are attached to a handle and shaken to make them clack against each other. Castanets do not have a definite pitch.

CELLO

A member of the string family that is about four feet tall. It is much lower in pitch than the violin. The cello, which is short for violoncello, rests on an end pin, and is held between the seated player's knees. With the right hand, the cellist draws the bow across the strings to produce the sound. By pressing on the string with the fingers of the left hand, the cellist changes pitch. There are 10 or 12 cellists in a full symphony orchestra.

CHIMES

A percussion instrument made of a number of finely tuned metal tubes hanging from a frame. The chimes player strikes the top of the tube with a wooden hammer to produce a ringing tone that is often used to imitate church bells. Also called tubular bells.

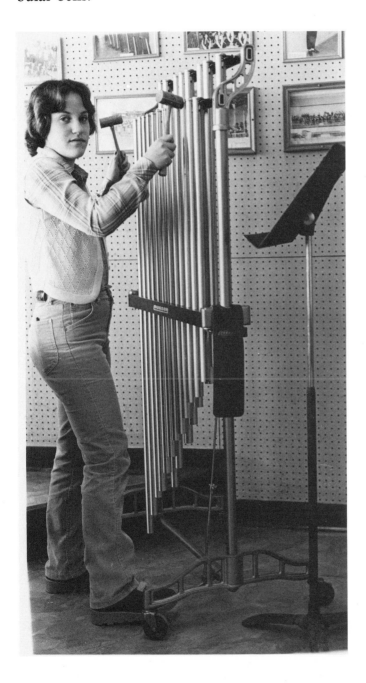

CLARINET

A woodwind instrument that produces its sound by means of a single reed clamped to the mouthpiece. By opening and closing holes, either with the fingers or by pressing keys, the clarinetist can play all the different notes. The 26-inch (66-centimeter) B-flat clarinet is the standard instrument. For some music, the slightly longer A clarinet is used. Special effects sometimes call for the much-shorter, higher-pitched E-flat clarinet. There are three or four clarinetists in an orchestra; one of them usually also plays the E-flat and bass clarinets.

CONCERT

A performance of music for an audience. The word, which comes from the Latin, means doing something together. Until the first public concerts, in the year 1672, music could only be heard in church or in the castles and palaces of nobles. Today more people attend concerts every year than baseball games. A concert given by one or two performers is called a recital.

oto courtesy London Symphony Orchestra

CONCERTMASTER/CONCERTMISTRESS

The first of the first violins. This player sits just to the conductor's left at the front of the stage. The concertmaster or concertmistress is the leader of the orchestra players and often helps the conductor at rehearsals. Sometimes called leader.

CONDUCTOR

The director of the orchestra. The conductor holds a short stick, called a baton, in the right hand, and uses it to beat time. The left hand indicates loudness and style and gives the musicians cues when they are to play. During rehearsals the conductor helps the players learn their parts, and makes sure that all the instruments are in proper balance and playing with the same feeling and expression.

Photo Eugene Netzer, courtesy National Orchestral Association

CONTRABASS. *See* Double Bass

CONTRABASSOON
A woodwind instrument similar to the bassoon that plays lower than all the other woodwinds and is one of the lowest pitched of all instruments. The 16-foot (4.9-meter) length of the contrabassoon is folded over four times, so that it is only about 4 feet (1.2 meters) tall. It ends in a bell that faces down. There is only one contrabassoon in an orchestra, and it is usually played by a bassoonist. Also called double bassoon.

CYMBAL

A plate-shaped brass disk about 15 inches (38 centimeters) in diameter and slightly concave in shape. Usually the cymbal is used in pairs. The player crashes the two cymbals against each other to produce the sound. The cymbal does not have a definite pitch.

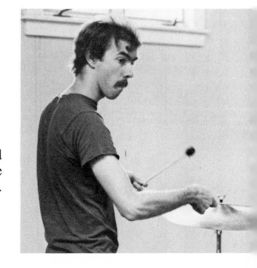

A single cymbal may be placed on a stand and played with one stick for separate strokes or two sticks for a sustained roll.

DOUBLE BASS

The lowest pitched string instrument. The double bass is played with the bassist standing or leaning on a stool. The bow is shorter and heavier than the bows used with other string instruments, and the distances the fingers of the left hand need to stretch are greater. There are nine double basses in a standard orchestra. Also called bass viol and contrabass.

DOUBLE BASSOON. *See* Contrabassoon

DRUMS

A group of percussion instruments of different diameters and depths with two plastic or hide heads stretched over a frame. Drums are played by striking one head, the batter head, with the drumstick or drumsticks. They do not produce notes of definite pitch.

The smallest is the snare or side drum, about 15 inches (38 centimeters) in diameter. Stretched across the bottom head are the snares, tight cords of metal or gut. When the batter head is struck, the snares vibrate against the bottom head, giving a sharp, brilliant sound. The snare drum is played with a pair of hard wooden sticks.

The middle-sized drum, the tenor drum, is just slightly larger than the snare, 17 inches (43 centimeters) in diameter. It is, however, much deeper than the snare drum and has no snares. The sound of the tenor drum is lower and darker than that of the snare drum. It is usually played with sticks that have soft, padded heads.

The largest drum of all is the bass drum. It is at least 32 inches (81 centimeters) in diameter. The two heads of the bass drum are thicker and looser than those of the other drums, and it has no snares. The bass drum is usually played with one very soft drumstick. Two or three musicians play the drums in most orchestras.

END PIN

The metal rod on which the cello and double bass rest. Players often sharpen the tip of the end pin with a metal file so it will not slip on the stage floor.

ENGLISH HORN

A woodwind instrument that is neither English nor a horn. The English horn is a large oboe with a double reed to produce the sound. Since it is longer than the oboe, its range extends five notes lower. The English horn is different from the oboe in that the reed is placed at the end of a curved metal tube and in that there is a pear-shaped bell at the bottom. There is one English horn in a symphony orchestra, usually played by an oboe player.

FLUTE

A high-pitched woodwind instrument. The player holds the flute across the chin and blows over a hole in the tube. By covering other holes and pressing on keys, the player is able to sound all the different notes. The flute is the only woodwind that is usually made of metal and that does not have a reed. Most full symphonies have two or three flute players, plus one who plays the piccolo (which is really a small flute).

FRENCH HORN

A brass instrument made up of a coil of thin brass tubing about 16 feet (4.9 meters) long, that flares out into a big bell at the end. The very first horns were actually animal horns that were used for hunting and signaling. Today's players produce the sound by buzzing their lips into the narrow cup mouthpiece. They change pitch by loosening or tightening their buzzing lips and by pressing the valves. Although there are only four different French horn parts in most orchestra music, there are often five or six horn players. The extra players sometimes take over for the first and third players, so that the regular players can be rested for the higher, more difficult parts they must play. Many musicians consider the French horn the hardest instrument of all to play well.

GLOCKENSPIEL

A percussion instrument consisting of a series of steel bars of varying lengths. The name is a German word meaning bell-play. By striking each of the bars of the glockenspiel with a hard mallet, the player is able to produce the bell-like tones of this instrument.

HARP

A plucked string instrument with 47 strings arranged in order from short to long. The harp was used in the early opera orchestras around the year 1600. After awhile, though, it fell from favor and was not part of the orchestra again until the middle of the 19th century. The player uses both hands to pluck the strings. A full symphony has one or two harps.

HARPSICHORD

A keyboard instrument that looks somewhat like a piano. When the player strikes a key on the harpsichord, one of the stretched strings inside the instrument is plucked (rather than struck with a felt hammer, as is the case in a piano). Some larger harpsichords have two different sets of strings with a separate keyboard for each set. The harpsichord is mostly used when the orchestra performs music of the 17th or 18th centuries. During that period, the harpsichord player often conducted the orchestra as well, while seated at the keyboard of the instrument.

KETTLEDRUM. *See* Timpani

LEADER. *See* Concertmaster

LIBRARIAN

The person in charge of the orchestra's music. The librarian gets the music for each program either from the orchestra's own library or from a supplier who rents or sells orchestral parts. It is the librarian's job to put the players' parts on the music stands before each rehearsal and concert and to collect them at the end.

MOUTHPIECE

The part of certain blowing instruments that is held in or against the player's mouth.

The clarinet mouthpiece is in the shape of a bird's beak. Players hold it between their lips.

Trombonists, and other brass players, insert the mouthpiece into the instrument before playing.

MUTE

A device placed in or on a string or brass instrument to soften and dampen the sound. Mutes used on the string instruments are rubber or wooden clamps that fit on the bridge, the upright piece of light wood on top of the instrument. The mute stops the bridge from vibrating freely and makes the sound softer, but it does not change the pitch of notes played.

Brass instrument mutes are inserted into the bell to cut the vibrations.

To get a "wah-wah" effect, the p[layer] waves a hand in front of certain typ[es of] brass instrument mutes.

OBOE

A woodwind instrument that produces its sound with a double reed. Originally the instrument was called *haut-bois,* which means high-wood in French. Over the centuries the name was changed to the Italian form, oboe. The oboe's pitch is controlled by opening and closing holes and pressing keys along its 21-inch (53.3-centimeter) length. There are two or three oboes in a full orchestra plus one more player for the English horn, a close relative of the oboe.

PERCUSSION

The family of instruments that produces sound by being hit or shaken. All percussion instruments may be divided into two groups: those with definite pitch, whose tones can be matched by other pitched instruments; and those without definite pitch, whose sounds cannot be matched. The most common pitched percussion instruments are the timpani, xylophone, glockenspiel, and chimes; others are the marimba and vibraphone. Among those without pitch, the most popular are the snare, tenor, and bass drums, cymbals, triangle, tambourine, and castanets; others are the gong, wood block, temple block, and rattle. There is usually one player for the timpani, and two or three players for all the other percussion instruments. The percussion players stand at the back of the stage, most often to the conductor's left.

Timpani

Glockenspiel, Cymbal

Snare Drum, Cymbals, Triangle, Bass Drum

PIANO

A keyboard instrument occasionally used in the orchestra. The name is short for pianoforte, which means soft-loud in Italian. The early pianos, built around the year 1700, were the first keyboard instruments that could play from soft to loud. Each time the player presses one of the 88 keys, a hammer strikes the string or strings inside the piano for that particular note, and the note is sounded. The piano is part of the string section because the sound is produced by a vibrating string. At the same time, it is part of the percussion family because the strings are set into vibration by being struck. There is only one piano in an orchestra.

PICCOLO

The smallest and highest-pitched woodwind instrument. The piccolo is also the smallest instrument in the orchestra. It is only 12½ inches (31.8 centimeters) long, about half the length of its close relative, the flute, and its range extends eight notes higher. It is played by blowing across a hole in the tubing and by covering holes or pressing the keys along its length. Both wooden and metal piccolos are used in orchestras. The single piccolo in most orchestras is usually played by a flutist.

PIT ORCHESTRA

A group of musicians, smaller than a full symphony, used to accompany operas, musical shows, dance performances, and other theatrical presentations. The pit orchestra usually plays in a space below floor level just in front of the stage that is called the pit.

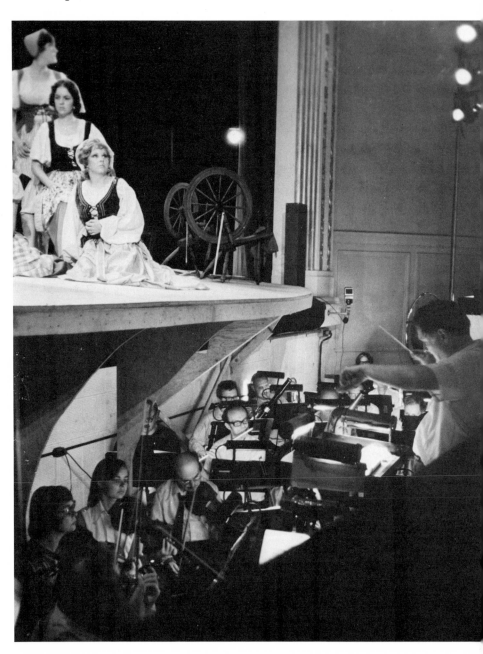

PIZZICATO

A way of playing a string instrument by plucking the strings with a finger instead of using a bow. *Pizzicato* is an Italian word that means pinched. The pizzicato effect is used on all string instruments.

RECORDING

Making a permanent copy of the sound of a musical performance. A number of microphones are used when recording an
orchestra. The microphones change the sounds of the musical
instruments into electrical impulses that are recorded on tape.
Later the tape is used to make both disk and tape recordings of
the music.

REED

The sound producer in all the woodwinds except the flute and piccolo. Reeds are made from a tall, stiff type of grass that grows around the Mediterranean Sea. The clarinet and saxophone use a single reed that vibrates against the mouthpiece. The oboe, English horn, bassoon, and contrabassoon use double reeds that vibrate against each other.

The oboe's double reed fits right into the top of the instrument. The player holds it between his or her lips.

REHEARSAL

The preparation for a concert. At rehearsals, the conductor leads the orchestra through the concert music and stops from time to time to work out any problems. The final rehearsal is often called the dress rehearsal. At this rehearsal the conductor tries to go straight through the entire program without stop to approximate concert conditions.

ROSIN

A substance that string players rub on the hair of their bows before they play. Rosin, which is made from turpentine, makes the hairs slightly sticky and helps to set the strings into vibration.

SAXOPHONE

An occasional member of the woodwind section of the orchestra. The saxophone is a favorite of jazz and pop music groups. First constructed in 1840 by Adolphe Sax and patented in 1846, the saxophone is really a cross between woodwind and brass instruments. The sound is produced by a single reed that is clamped to the mouthpiece much like that of the clarinet. The instrument itself, though, is made of brass like the trumpet and trombone.

SIDE DRUM. *See* Drums

SNARE DRUM. *See* Drums

SOLOIST

An instrumentalist or singer who performs a solo work with orchestra. Instrumental soloists usually play works called concertos. Singers either perform selections from operas, called arias, or special compositions written for vocalist and orchestra.

The soloist usually stands to the conductor's left, between the conductor and the first violins. When there is a piano soloist, the instrument and performer are located behind the conductor as he faces the orchestra.

SOUSAPHONE. *See* Tuba

STAND PARTNERS
Two players in an orchestra who share the same music stand and music. The performer towards the back of the stage is responsible for turning pages.

Photo Eugene Netzer,
courtesy National Orchestral Association

STRINGS

The largest family in a full orchestra, with over 60 players. The strings include the violins, violas, cellos, and double basses. The sound is produced by a vibrating string. The player pulls the bow across the string to set it into vibration. Then, by pressing on the string with the fingers of the left hand, the player changes the vibrating length of the string and thereby changes the notes. The string instrument players are on the front part of the stage. To the conductor's left the 18 first violins are closest to the audience, and the 16 second violins are towards the center of the stage. To the conductor's right, the 12 cellos are on the outside and the 12 violas are towards the center, although their positions are sometimes reversed. The nine double basses are in a line behind the cellos and violas along the right side of the stage. The harp is also a string instrument. It is usually considered separately, though, because it is plucked, rather than played with a bow.

Violins

Violas

Cellos

Double Basses

TAMBOURINE

A percussion instrument made of a single head with a 10- to 12-inch (25.4- to 30.5-centimeter) diameter. The tambourine head is stretched over a 3-inch (7.6-centimeter) deep wooden hoop. Set into the hoop are metal disks that produce a jingling sound when they hit each other. The tambourine is an ancient instrument that has changed hardly at all over the centuries. Remains of tambourines from ancient Rome look just like modern ones. The tambourine is played either by striking the head, by shaking, or by running a thumb around the edge, which gives a rapid, continuing jingle sound. Neither the head nor the jingles produce a definite pitch.

TENOR DRUM. *See* Drums

TIMPANI

The most important instrument of the percussion group. Timpani are made of large, hollow copper "kettles," with a plastic drumhead stretched over the top. They originated in the Mideast, where soldiers mounted on horses or camels had pairs of these drums to beat loudly as they rode into battle. The timpani are the only drums that can produce notes of definite pitch. Most orchestras use three or four timpani with diameters from 21 to 31 inches (53.3 to 78.7 centimeters) to get a full range of notes. The player uses pairs of sticks with either soft padded heads or hard wooden heads to obtain different musical effects. Also called kettledrums.

TRIANGLE

A percussion instrument made of a steel rod bent into the shape of a triangle left open at one angle. The player holds the triangle by a string looped through the upper angle and strikes it with a metal beater. The triangle has a high-pitched ringing sound with no definite pitch.

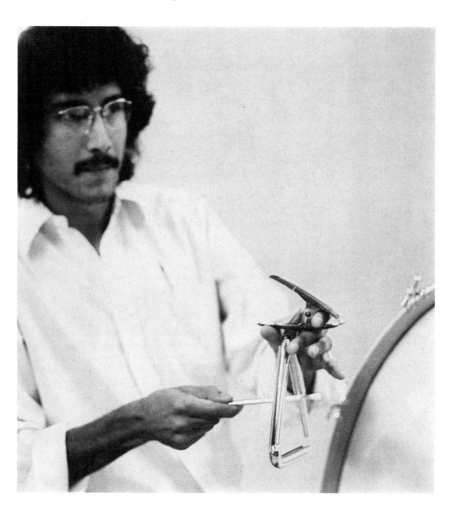

TROMBONE

A low-pitched brass instrument. The trombone is the only member of the brass family with a slide, which is a long, narrow, U-shaped length of tubing. The ancestor of the trombone was the sackbut, from the French word, *sacqueboute,* which means pull-tube. The player moves the slide back and forth to change pitch. The sound is created as the player blows, setting the lips into vibration in the cup-shaped mouthpiece. There are three or four trombones in the typical orchestra.

TRUMPET

The highest-pitched brass instrument. The original trumpet was simply a hollow tree branch or a bamboo stem that became, over the centuries, the most important instrument for military and ceremonial use. The trumpet player's buzzing lips in the mouthpiece create the basic sound. Changing the buzzing and pressing the valves allows the player to change pitch and play all the notes in the music. The standard instrument is the B-flat trumpet, though there are both bigger and smaller members of the trumpet family. Most trumpet players have a number of different size instruments so that they can use the very best one for the music they are playing. There are usually three trumpets in an orchestra.

TUBA

The largest and lowest sounding brass instrument. The tuba player's buzzing lips in the mouthpiece produce the sound. Adjusting the tightness of the lips and pressing the valves lets the player perform the music written for the instrument. The tuba rests on the player's lap. Occasionally the sousaphone (named for John Philip Sousa), another type of tuba, is used. The big sousaphone bell can be turned to face in any direction instead of only pointing up, as the tuba does. There is only one tuba player in an orchestra.

TUBULAR BELLS. *See* Chimes

TUNING

Adjusting the instruments so that they are all at the same pitch. Orchestra musicians usually tune before every rehearsal and concert and in between the different selections as well. They usually tune to the note A sounded by the oboe. String players tune their instruments by turning the pegs to which the strings are attached. By tightening the strings, they raise the pitch. By loosening the strings, they lower the pitch.

The woodwind and brass players tune
their instruments by shortening or lengthening the tubing of their instruments.

The timpanist tunes by using a foot pedal
to tighten or loosen the head of the timpani. Bending over the drum makes it
easier to hear the pitch clearly.

VIOLA

A string instrument that looks very much like the violin, but is slightly larger, giving it a darker tone, and allowing its range to extend five notes lower. The viola, as well as the other strings, is made of spruce wood for the top and curly maple for the back. The violist uses the bow to set the strings into vibration and presses on the strings with the fingers of the left hand to play all the different notes. A full viola section has 12 players.

VIOLIN

The smallest string instrument and the highest in pitch. The violin rests under the player's chin and is held up by the left hand. The player draws the bow across the strings with the right hand to set them into vibration and produce the sound. By pressing down on the strings with the fingers of the left hand, the player shortens the vibrating lengths and changes the pitch. The violins are divided into two sections. There are up to 18 first violins. They usually play the higher melody parts. The second violins, with about 16 players, have a lower line and play the accompaniment more often. The first violins sit at the front of the stage on the conductor's left; the second violins sit next to them toward the back of the stage.

VIOLONCELLO. *See* Cello

WOODWINDS

A family of blowing instruments that were originally all made of wood. Today the oboe, clarinet, and bassoon are still made of wood, but most modern flutes are made of metal. All the woodwinds, except the flute, are played by blowing past a reed or two reeds, which sets the air inside the instrument into vibration. The flutist blows across a hole to start the air vibrating. The body of each woodwind instrument is a hollow tube with holes cut into it. The player produces different notes by opening and closing these holes, either with fingers or by using the metal keys.

Each of the main woodwinds, flute, oboe, clarinet, and bassoon, has a related instrument that is also part of the orchestra. The piccolo is a small relative of the flute. The English horn is a large oboe. The bass clarinet is a longer, thicker version of the standard B-flat clarinet. And the contrabassoon is a much bigger, lower-pitched bassoon.

A full symphony orchestra has from 12 to 16 woodwinds. They sit close to the center of the stage in two rows. The flutes and oboes are in the front row; the clarinets and bassoons are right behind them.

Flutes

Oboes

Clarinets

Bassoons

XYLOPHONE

A percussion instrument with a separate length of wood for each of the notes. The name comes from the Greek *xylos* meaning wood and *phone* meaning sound. The xylophone is played with two mallets that have hard heads. The xylophone is high in pitch. When it is played loudly it can be heard over the entire orchestra.